ACTIVE PURRSUITS

Viv Quillin

VICTOR GOLLANCZ • LONDON

First published in Great Britain 1995
by Victor Gollancz
An imprint of the Cassell Group
Wellington House, 125 Strand, London WCR 0BB

A catalogue record for this book is available from the British Library.
ISBN 0 575 05895 1

Designed by Robert Updegraff
Printed in Hong Kong by Wing King Tong Company Limited

To Bob, with love

WARMING UP

It is vital to begin any sporting activity with a thorough warm-up session. Some cats consider this aspect *so* important that they never do anything else.

PICKING THE TEAM

Remember, *someone* has to be the
last cat to get picked.

A close-knit team
is always the most
effective.

FOOTBALL

Tips
1. After kicking another player on the leg . . .

. . . quickly throw yourself on the ground and miaow in agony.

Kit
Sturdy boots
Shin protectors
Snack (for half time)

Rules
Five minutes play at each end, with a forty-five minute rest break in the middle.

2. *Never* trip *anyone* up . . . when the referee is watching.

3. Very clever, but is it *effective* goalkeeping?

4. When dribbling try not to soak the ball as it slows the game down.

CRICKET

Bowling

Tiger Lily, a two-year-old Shorthair from Slough, is renowned for his unusual slow-bowling approach . . .

Batting

Heather, an attractive blue-eyed Persian from Dundee, has scored a record number of runs in her career and has also twice clocked up a litter of kittens in the lunch break.

Wicketkeeping

Never forget that your ability to sire kittens is not as important as your ability to eat dinner.

Slip Fielding

Try to resist this golden opportunity to catch up on your bottom-sniffing quota.

Deep Fielding

Possibly the most sought-after position in the game – with only the drone of bees to distract one's *total* attention from the job in hand.

NETBALL

Netball has long been established as a very suitable game for the female cat. It requires grace, agility and imaginative use of the knicker.

Procedure

1. Run very fast until you get the ball, then stop.

2. Throw the ball at someone else . . .

3. . . . or make a goal by putting the ball through the net.

Marcia scores, despite a magnificent defence.

ICE HOCKEY

Only plentiful supplies of electric blankets and hot-water bottles will lure the average cat on to the ice. Goalkeepers need especial protection from the cold.

The Sin Bin

Players infringing the rules have to spend time in the penalty box. Two minutes for charging another cat, five minutes for fighting. (The most innocent-looking cats are often the naughtiest.)

Procedure
Try to hit the puck into the *goal*.

AMERICAN FOOTBALL

The popularity of this tough game has spread world wide, not least amongst cats, that well-known species of rough-and-tumble, hard-bitten roisterers.

With all his equipment on, this Tunbridge Wells Tiger looks quite intimidating . . .

. . . but underneath it's still Fluffy from Number 11 Pine Walk.

The West Drayton Goldfish are a new team – and still saving up for the correct protective gear.

WATER SPORTS

Getting wet is the last thing most cats want to do.

It is possible to overcome this phobia by immersing *small* portions of oneself in water for brief periods.

Unfortunately these heroic efforts are often misunderstood by one's owner.

Baam!

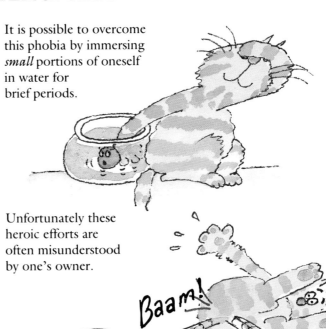

. . . Once the fear of water has been overcome there is nothing more boring than the water show-off.

Canoeing

Equipment
Canoe
Paddle
Water

For the average food-fixated feline the pay-offs of becoming a water lover are enormous . . .

Equipment
You will need a life jacket, air tank and flippers. Also a spear and store for catch, if you are fishing. Any old household utensils can be used as swimming apparatus. They will almost certainly be ineffective.

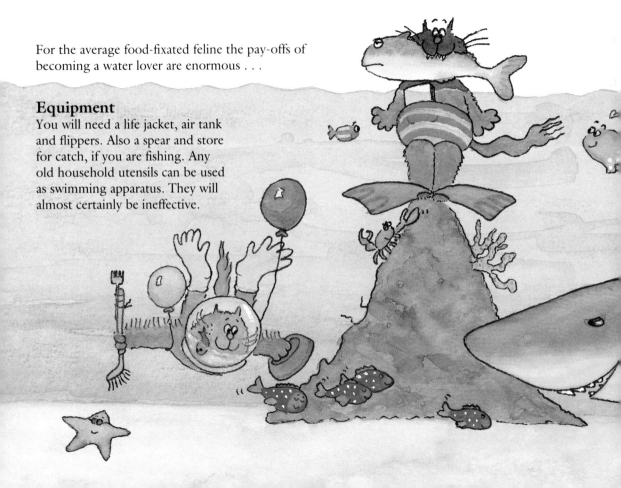

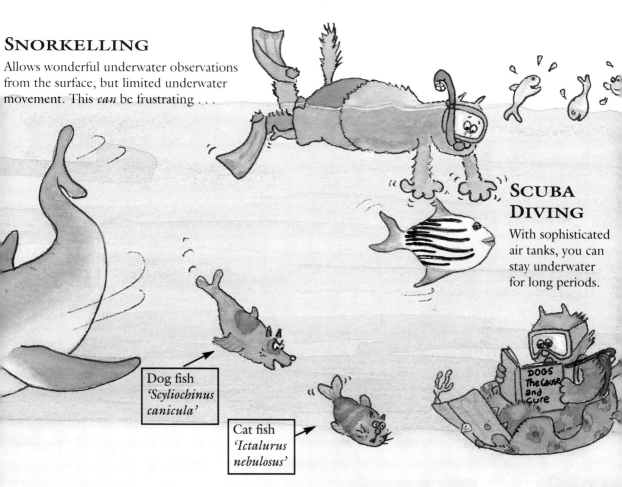

SNORKELLING

Allows wonderful underwater observations from the surface, but limited underwater movement. This *can* be frustrating . . .

SCUBA DIVING

With sophisticated air tanks, you can stay underwater for long periods.

Dog fish
'Scyliochinus canicula'

Cat fish
'Ictalurus nebulosus'

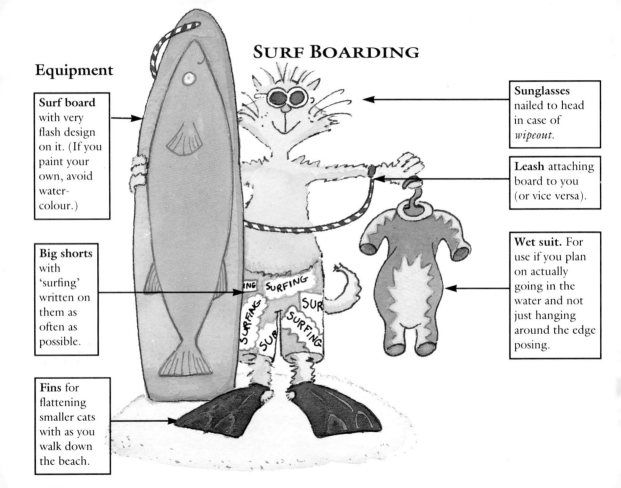

Surf Boarding

Equipment

Surf board with very flash design on it. (If you paint your own, avoid water-colour.)

Big shorts with 'surfing' written on them as often as possible.

Fins for flattening smaller cats with as you walk down the beach.

Sunglasses nailed to head in case of *wipeout*.

Leash attaching board to you (or vice versa).

Wet suit. For use if you plan on actually going in the water and not just hanging around the edge posing.

1. Using your front paws, paddle well out to the big waves.

Method

2. Turn around and paddle back until a wave picks you up, and then jump on to your board. (This takes practice.)

3. Enjoy the exhilarating experience of being carried back to the beach.

SYNCHRONIZED SWIMMING

Art in a cozzie.

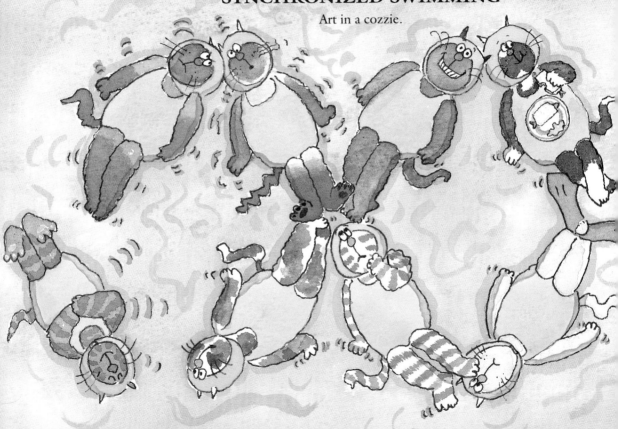

SYNCHRONIZED SWIMMING UNDERWATER

Once you have learnt to hold your breath, as long as your
tail is in the right position, your time is your own.

SAILING

There is nothing quite so jolly as feeling the wind howling up your jumper
and the water spraying on your face as you race along.

Procedure
1. Launch your boat.

2. Lean well out over the side.

3. Check that the crew is concentrating, by tacking without warning.

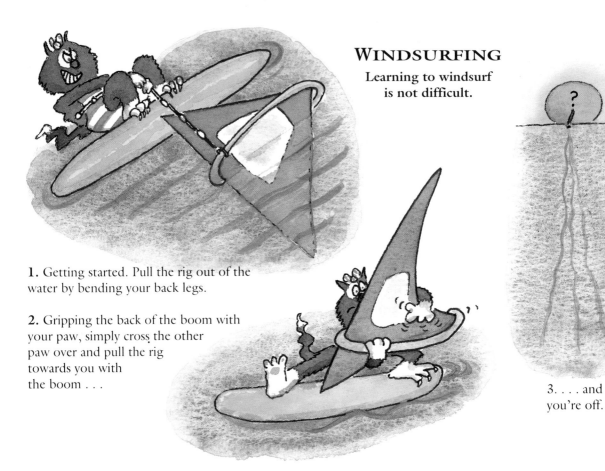

WINDSURFING

**Learning to windsurf
is not difficult.**

1. Getting started. Pull the rig out of the
water by bending your back legs.

2. Gripping the back of the boom with
your paw, simply cross the other
paw over and pull the rig
towards you with
the boom . . .

3. . . . and
you're off.

Funboarding

Involves leaping from a wave into the air and turning right over. One often lands upside down or falls off the sail board altogether. Obviously this is a lot of fun.

Freestyle

This is like gymnastics on a sail board. Olga performs the *splits* whilst railroading with a *tail plunge* thrown in for good measure.

FISHING

For the Seriously Committed Fishercat

Equipment
Hamper
Waders
Bait box
Keep net
Umbrella
Landing net
Tackle boxes
Folding seat
Rods
Reels
Hooks
Floats
Lines
Weights
Spare
hamper

And don't forget to put on some fish repellent.

The Amateur Has a Much Easier Time

1. Fine days.

2. Not such fine days.

Nothing can beat the satisfaction of cooking fish over an open fire that you have built yourself.

Sports for Cats Who Like Being Pushed, Thumped or Squashed

Sumo Wrestling

Ancient Japanese sport requiring large amounts of politeness *before* you tear your opponent apart, and a big thank-you afterwards. (In fact Sumo requires large amounts of *everything* so eat your hearts out, dieters.)

Gyoji, or referee checking all is in order before the contest. (A popular job for the keen bottom-sniffer.)

WRESTLING

The beginner should pick an inanimate object to practise on as there is less likelihood of losing an ear or being bitten . . .

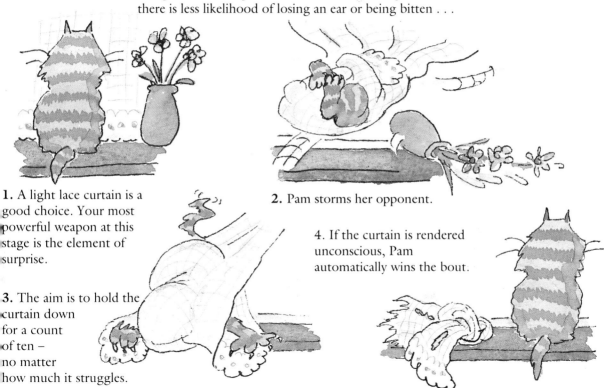

1. A light lace curtain is a good choice. Your most powerful weapon at this stage is the element of surprise.

2. Pam storms her opponent.

3. The aim is to hold the curtain down for a count of ten – no matter how much it struggles.

4. If the curtain is rendered unconscious, Pam automatically wins the bout.

BOXING

Procedure
1. Ignore each other
and slowly twitch tails.

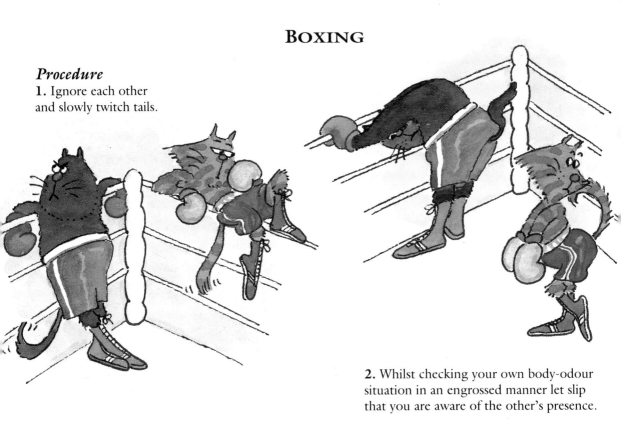

2. Whilst checking your own body-odour
situation in an engrossed manner let slip
that you are aware of the other's presence.

5. When you have had enough, admit defeat by walking off, licking yourself nonchalantly.

3. Spit, hiss and boo at each other, then run away fast unless you really want a fight.

4. Too late.

PROFESSIONAL TENNIS

The champions train for years, and they begin their careers younger and younger.

Procedure

1. Start practising as early as possible for working close up to the net.

Joyce needs more speed with her reflex actions.

2. Kittens often need a *double*-paw grip for an *effective* smash stroke.

Fifi and Fluffikins have developed a surprisingly powerful *follow-through*.

Really keen parents encourage their offspring to play tennis *before* they learn to walk.

TENNIS

Star tips on how the top players keep ahead:

★ Stripy's top-spin serve is feared on the Toms Tournament.

★ See the way Fluffy Grath always anticipates the next shot.

✭ Martina Natcattylova executes a difficult ball.

✭ Smoky uses the lob to devastating effect.

GYMNASTICS

All cats can *enjoy* gymnastics,
but to win medals you need to be . . . thin

. . . short

. . . and almost
nauseatingly cute.

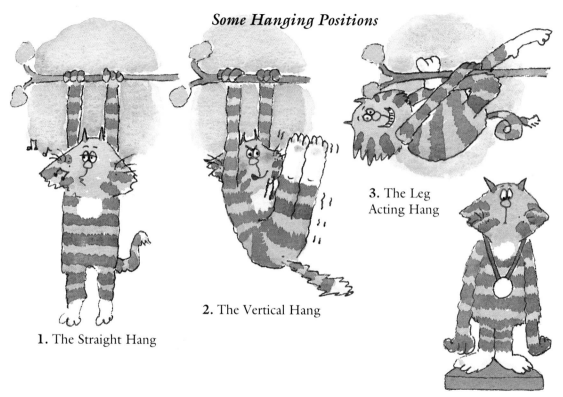

Some Hanging Positions

1. The Straight Hang

2. The Vertical Hang

3. The Leg Acting Hang

4. The Gold Medal Hang

Mounting

1. With the reins in the left front paw, grasp the stirrup with the right front paw . . .

2. . . . and with the left *back* paw in the stirrup spring lightly on to the horse.

Equipment
Horse

Maintenance
You cannot simply slap a fresh coat of paint on a horse in the spring to keep it in good working order. A horse needs regular grooming.

The Trot

A bumpy trip, and the rider should . . .   . . . stand and sit alternately.

The Canter

The rider should sit upright or, for a fast canter, lean forward in a comfortable, relaxed position.

The Gallop

Handy tip. Using claws to hang on to a runaway horse will probably make things worse.

SPORTING INJURIES

Squashed Paws

With a large number of paws on the move, obviously the risk of being trodden on cannot be overlooked. The excruciating pain which follows can only be guessed at by anyone who is not a cat.

Migraine

An increasing hazard in sport as more and more lurid colours are introduced. This cat is suffering from *Trouser Glare*. Dark glasses will help, but do nothing to eradicate the problem of appalling fashion sense.

Massage

Can be very helpful, but unfortunately far too many felines seem to think they need stroking every five minutes – even when there is nothing wrong with them.

ATHLETIC SPORTS CLINIC

(Polite name for pointing out all your really stupid mistakes.)

Sprinting

Fault. Poor concentration.

Fiona got off to a good start but was distracted by an interesting smell.
Hot Tip. Wear a nose clip.

Discus Throw

Fault. Incorrect swing.

Derek has created a vortex, due to leading into the turn with his shoulders.
Hot Tip. Run like hell before he lets go of the discus.

Hurdling

Fault. Inability to clear hurdles.

Basil's brilliant technique will never fully compensate for his short legs.
Hot Tip. Retrain as a jockey or footstool.

Javelin Throw

Fault. Wrong grip.

Simone is gripping the javelin like a handle making proper delivery impossible.
Hot Tip. Remember to *let go*.

THE PSYCHOLOGY OF WINNING

Psyching yourself to the top.

1. Instantly feel superior to your opponent by imagining him/her without clothes on.

2. Improve your concentration by separating your personal life from the game as much as possible.

3. Never admit you are beaten. Keep going back for more.

4. Remember to enjoy the rewards of success.

DISCOVER YOUR PERSONALITY BY THE SPORT YOU PREFER

For instance: Perhaps you are the boring type and have no friends. Long distance running would suit you . . . probably in the Ruislip area.

TABLE TENNIS

Personality

The gourmet who enjoys leisurely exercise with frequent pauses to enjoy a little soupçon of something.

NB. Not to be confused with 'Ping Pong', a lightning game of speed for the professional.

RUGBY

Size is an advantage in this game

Personality
The cat who likes to blend into its surroundings.

Any quarrels are soon made up in the communal bath after the game.

The referee must have integrity . . . and also know when to back down.

GOLF

Personalities

The big cats who run the neighbourhood will all be seen plotting on the golf course. Would-be gang leaders often offer to caddy.

Equipment

Loud trousers
Hairy skirts
Weird shoes
Plus some golf clubs

Playing An Uphill Lie
The main problem is your balance. The ball tends to fly quite high on this shot . . .

. . . you may even hit a birdie.

✫ *Star Tip*
Jack Nick-Claws takes plenty of time to think a shot through before playing it.

QUIET

SQUASH

Personality

The Go-Getter. This cat will go for anything that moves whether or not there is any hope of catching it.

Technique

Tinker is famous for his brilliant service.

The Options
Hard hitting is not everything . . .
Frank plays an angle with great delicacy.

Court Craft
Trish delivers a straight hit which
devastates the opposition.

ROLLER BLADING

Personality

The lean, keen feline of the nineties who wants to join the *fast* lane, ROLLER BLADES can do it for you!

1. Roger, a professional sprinter, is putting his best paw forwards . . . But Fluffy (an air-head from Anglesey) easily overtakes him on her ROLLER BLADES.

2. Anita Brown, an ambitious office worker from Luton, steps up efficiency with ROLLER BLADES.

3. Head for the heights and exercise on the way up . . . like Tracy, who is coming up against the ROLLER BLADE equivalent of the 'glass ceiling'.

4. . . . and, finally, use those precious minutes gained by ROLLER BLADES . . . to relax.

SHOOTING

Personality

The Natural Hunter. Nothing and no one is safe from this cat's instinct to stalk and destroy anything that moves. Often gives things that *don't* move a good going over just to show them who's boss.

The urge to kill can be channelled into harmless
sports such as claydog shooting or the rifle range.

BIRD WATCHING

Personality
The Introvert. Tends to seek closeness with those who avoid intimacy.

Procedure
The aim is to get as close as possible to your ~~prey~~ subject without being noticed.

1. Disguise. Clever use of natural materials will enable you to approach unnoticed.

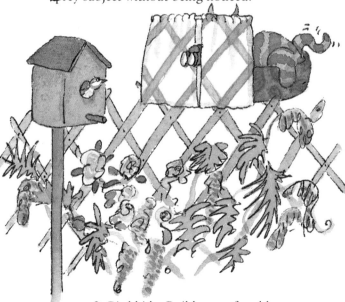

2. Bird hide. Build a comfortable, yet inconspicuous, hiding place close to the nesting area.

Being a bird watcher can be much more strenuous than you'd expect . . .

. . . not to mention frustrating.

CYCLING

Personality

The Totally Sedentary Cat. Cycling may seem a surprising activity to go for, but if you book the back seat on a tandem you need do nothing more than utter a few heavy groans and sighs on the uphill slog. Try not to eat the *entire* picnic en route.

Equipment
Tight, shiny shorts
Tandem
Trusting fellow cyclist
Knitting, or a relaxing book

Downhill Cycling

The only effort involved here is in staying awake. At the bottom of the hill, either phone for your car or ...

... run into something which renders your bike unridable. Using piteous miaows attract a lift by car or ...

... a crossbar with another cyclist (see tandem).

BOWLS

Personality

This activity suits the *laid-back* cat. The observer who enjoys watching life go by. The feline who jumps on anything that moves would cause havoc in a game of bowls.

Even as a kitten Basil never tired of watching his owners throw things.

He particularly enjoyed their skill in *fetching* the objects.

The length of time they would play before getting bored really impressed him.

Dress Code

The entire outfit should be *white*, excepting the footwear which is *flat* and brown.

If you don't possess a white ensemble, borrow one.

Some cats never *quite* lose the urge to chase the bowl.

DRUGS AND BRIBES

It's no use pretending these problems don't exist. As long as Catnip is sold openly at garden centres, and felines are kept short of pocket money, the issues won't go away.

Here is the now famous commentary from the Little Piddlington versus Netherbottom croquet final:

'Monica Braithwaite has keeled over and appears to have fallen *asleep*! I admit it's been a boring game but no competitor has ever dozed off before whilst playing a key shot. It has to be asked – *was she drugged or did someone pay her to take a dive?*'

Monica's Trainer

Roger arousing suspicion with his record-breaking start to the 100-metre sprint . . .

'. . . and on closer inspection of the video replay we can see clearly that a can of flea spray has been used. This is a banned drug for its known effect of causing cats to run at artificially induced high speeds. Roger is *disqualified*.'

Roger (a long-haired Maine Coone) claimed to have a fur problem with unwanted guests. 'I didn't want to slow down my performance by scratching,' he said. 'I'm innocent.'

SPORTS FOR THE SUICIDAL
OR FOOLHARDY CAT

Sometimes life just doesn't seem worth living (perhaps
you have lost your tin opener). Or you are bored,
bored, *bored*, and need an injection of excitement.

BUNGEE JUMPING

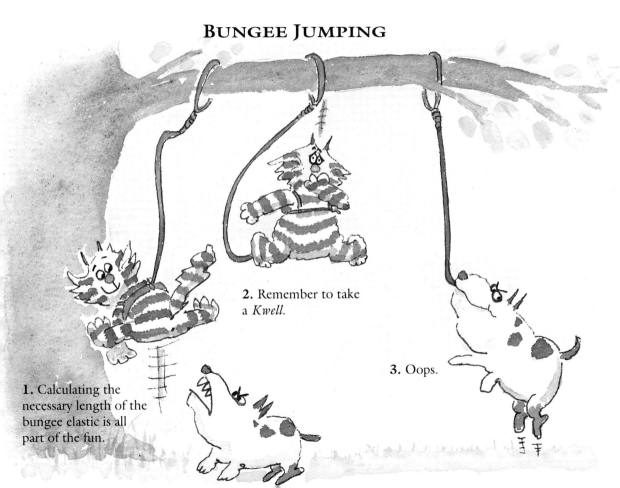

1. Calculating the necessary length of the bungee elastic is all part of the fun.

2. Remember to take a *Kwell*.

3. Oops.

Norman surveys the North Face of the curtains. Oxygen will be needed above pelmet level.

CLIMBING

1. The going can be tough but the rewards are worth it . . .

2. . . . although the risk of avalanche is never far away.

Fluffy, Snowy and Clive bivouac overnight with only seventeen tins of sardines between them.

Why Climb?
'Because it's there,' says Andrea, who has successfully conquered every aspect of her owners' hessian wallpaper.

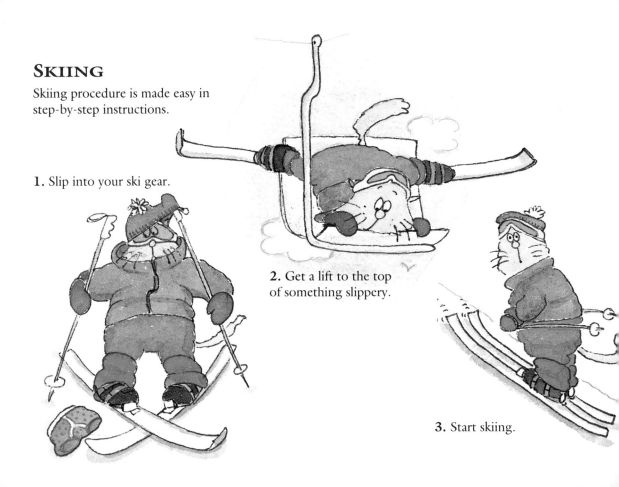

SKIING

Skiing procedure is made easy in step-by-step instructions.

1. Slip into your ski gear.

2. Get a lift to the top of something slippery.

3. Start skiing.

4. Go very fast.

5. Stop.

PARACHUTING

Equipment
Aeroplane or cliff top
Parachute
Smallish hamper
Spare set of underwear

Procedure
1. Practise jumping off short things . . .

2. . . . then taller things. A kitchen work top is *ideal* for this.

Good equipment can make the difference between going home for tea afterwards and . . . not going home for tea afterwards.

It *is* possible to *knit* your own parachute, but the air goes through the holes frighteningly fast (particularly if using a lacy pattern).

✸ *Star Tip*
'If you're going to jump, *jump*,' says Biggles, a veteran Shorthair with artificial paws.

SPECTATOR SPORTS

All sports are enhanced by the roar of encouragement
from an enthusiastic, attentive audience.

CRICKET

This is a *marvellous* spectator sport as one is not only able to catnap for a couple of hours, safe in the knowledge that one is unlikely to miss anything, but there's an awfully good tea (with a heavy emphasis on *dairy produce*) to be had in the pavilion afterwards.

THE AUTHOR

Viv Quillin was born in the Pennines, where sport is compulsory to ward off hypothermia. She is the author of several books, including *Mother Always Said* and *Pussyfooting*, which examine the strange yet fascinating behaviour of mothers and cats (more or less in that order). Her cartoons have also appeared in the *Evening Standard*, *Spare Rib*, *Cosmopolitan* and the *New Internationalist*, as well as on postcards, and have been translated into many different languages.

In the hope of acquiring a more cultured sense of humour, she moved to Oxford in 1988.